OIL SPILL COSTS AND IMPACTS

Oil Spill Costs and Impacts

Robert H. Urwellen

Nova Science Publishers, Inc.
New York

For permission to use material from this book please contact us:
Telephone 631-231-7269; Fax 631-231-8175
Web Site: http://www.novapublishers.com

NOTICE TO THE READER

The Publisher has taken reasonable care in the preparation of this book, but makes no expressed or implied warranty of any kind and assumes no responsibility for any errors or omissions. No liability is assumed for incidental or consequential damages in connection with or arising out of information contained in this book. The Publisher shall not be liable for any special, consequential, or exemplary damages resulting, in whole or in part, from the readers' use of, or reliance upon, this material.

Independent verification should be sought for any data, advice or recommendations contained in this book. In addition, no responsibility is assumed by the publisher for any injury and/or damage to persons or property arising from any methods, products, instructions, ideas or otherwise contained in this publication.

This publication is designed to provide accurate and authoritative information with regard to the subject matter covered herein. It is sold with the clear understanding that the Publisher is not engaged in rendering legal or any other professional services. If legal or any other expert assistance is required, the services of a competent person should be sought. FROM A DECLARATION OF PARTICIPANTS JOINTLY ADOPTED BY A COMMITTEE OF THE AMERICAN BAR ASSOCIATION AND A COMMITTEE OF PUBLISHERS.

LIBRARY OF CONGRESS CATALOGING-IN-PUBLICATION DATA

Urwellen, Robert H.
    Oil Spill costs and impacts/Robert H. Urwellen.
        p.cm.
    Includes index.
    ISBN: 978-1-60692-119-7 (softcover)
    1.   Oil spills—Economic aspects. 2. Oil spills—Environmental aspects. 1. Title.
    TD427.P4U79 2009
    363.738'2—dc22
                                        2008055221

Published by Nova Science Publishers, Inc. ✝ *New York*

CONTENTS

PREFACE

When oil spills occur in U.S. waters, federal law places primary liability on the vessel owner or operator—that is, the responsible party—up to a statutory limit. As a supplement to this "polluter pays" approach, a federal Oil Spill Liability Trust Fund administered by the Coast Guard pays for costs when a responsible party does not or cannot pay.

This book is based on a GAO report on oil spill costs and select program updates on the recent San Francisco spill. Specifically, it answers three questions: (1) How many major spills (i.e., at least $1 million) have occurred since 1990, and what is their total cost? (2) What factors affect the cost of spills? and (3) What are the implications of major oil spills for the Oil Spill Liability Trust Fund?

MAJOR OIL SPILLS OCCUR INFREQUENTLY, BUT RISKS REMAIN

STATEMENT OF SUSAN A. FLEMING, DIRECTOR PHYSICAL INFRASTRUCTURE ISSUES[*]

Madame Chair and Members of the Subcommittee:

We appreciate the opportunity to be here today to discuss the costs of major oil spills. As the recent accident in San Francisco Bay illustrates, the potential for an oil spill exists daily across coastal and inland waters of the United States. Specifically, on November 7, 2007, a cargo ship leaving the Port of Oakland struck the San Francisco-Oakland Bay Bridge, tearing the hull of the ship. As a result, over 50,000 gallons of heavy oil spilled into the bay [1]. The total cost of cleaning up the spill, as well as the damage to marine wildlife and fisheries is still undetermined. As this spill also illustrates, the potential for costly spills is present for vessels other than tankers and tank barges involved in the petroleum industry. Cargo, fishing, and other types of vessels also carry substantial fuel reserves and accidents can release this fuel and create substantial damage. Spills can be expensive, with considerable costs to the federal government and the private sector.

The framework for addressing and paying for maritime oil spills is identified in the Oil Pollution Act of 1990 (OPA), which was enacted after the Exxon Valdez spill. OPA created a "polluter pays" system that places the primary burden of liability and the costs of oil spills on the vessel owner or operator who was

---

[*] Excerpted from GAO Report 08-357T, dated December 18, 2007.

responsible for the spill—that is, the responsible party. However, there are financial limitations on that liability. Under this system, the responsible party assumes, up to a specified limit, the burden of paying for spill costs—which can include both removal costs (cleaning up the spill) and damage claims (restoring the environment and payment of compensation to parties that were economically harmed by the spill). Above the specified limit, the responsible party is no longer financially liable [2]. To pay costs above the limit of liability, as well as to pay costs when a responsible party does not pay or cannot be identified, OPA authorized the Oil Spill Liability Trust Fund (Fund), which is financed primarily from a per-barrel tax on petroleum products either produced in the United States or imported from other countries. The Fund is administered by the National Pollution Funds Center (NPFC) within the U.S. Coast Guard. The balance in the Fund— about $600 million at the end of fiscal year 2006—is well below its peak of $1.2 billion in 2000. The decline in the Fund's balance primarily reflects an expiration of the barrel tax on petroleum in 1994. The tax was not reinstated until 2005.

While this system is well understood, the costs involved in responding to oil spills are less clear. Costs paid from the Fund are well documented, but the party responsible for the spill is not required to report the costs it incurs. As a result, private-sector and total costs for cleaning up spills and paying damages are largely unknown to the public. The lack of information about the cost of spills, the declining Fund balance, and significant claims made on the Fund—for spills in which the removal costs and damage claims have exceeded established OPA. liability limits—have all raised concerns about the Fund's long-term viability.

Although we have not assessed the November 2007 San Francisco oil spill in depth, we have done considerable work looking at the cost of major spills in recent years and the factors that contribute to making spills particularly expensive to clean up and mitigate. My remarks today are intended to provide a context for looking at the nation's approach to paying the costs of such spills. Specifically, my testimony today focuses on (1) the number of major oil spills—i.e., spills for which the total costs and claims paid was at least $1 million—from 1990 to 2006 and the total costs of these spills, (2) the factors that affect major oil spill costs, and (3) the implications of major oil spill costs for the Oil Spill Liability Trust Fund [3]. My comments are based primarily on our September 2007 report on oil spill costs, which was issued to the Senate Committee on Commerce, Science, and Transportation and the House Committee on Transportation and Infrastructure [4]. In preparing our September report, we analyzed oil spill removal cost and claims data from NPFC, the National Oceanic and Atmospheric Administration's (NOAA) Damage Assessment, Remediation and Restoration Program, and the

Department of the Interior's (DOI) Natural Resource Damage Assessment and Restoration Program and the U.S. Fish and Wildlife Service (FWS). We also analyzed cost data obtained from vessel insurers and through contract with Environmental Research Consulting [5]. We interviewed NPFC, NOAA, and state officials responsible for oil spill response, as well as industry experts and representatives from key industry associations and a vessel owner. In addition, we selected five oil spills on the basis of the spill's location, oil type, and spill volume for an in-depth review. During this review, we interviewed NPFC officials involved in spill response for all five spills, as well as representatives of private sector companies involved in the spill and spill response; and we conducted a file review of NPFC records of the federal oil spill removal activities and costs associated with spill cleanup. We also reviewed documentation from the NPFC regarding the Fund balance and vessels' limits of liability. Because private-sector and total costs for cleaning up spills and paying damages are not centrally tracked and maintained, we obtained the best available cost data from a variety of sources, as previously described. We then combined the information that we collected from these various sources to develop cost estimates for the oil spills. However, because the cost data are somewhat imprecise and the data we collected vary somewhat by source, we present the cost estimates in ranges. The lower and higher bounds of the range represent the low and high end of cost information we obtained. Based on reviews of data documentation, interviews with relevant officials, and tests for reasonableness, we determined that the data were sufficiently reliable for the purposes of our report. We also conducted additional research and interviewed NPFC officials to update our September 2007 report's findings and to gather information on the recent oil spill in San Francisco Bay. We conducted this work in December 2007 in accordance with generally accepted government auditing standards.

SUMMARY

We estimate that from 1990 to 2006, 51 oil spills have involved removal costs and damage claims totaling at least $1 million. Collectively, from public and nonpublic sources, we estimate that responsible parties and the Fund have paid between approximately $860 million and $1.1 billion to clean up these spills and compensate affected parties. Responsible parties paid between about 72 to 78 percent of these costs; the Fund has paid the remainder, or $240 million. The overall cost for the 51 spills we identified could also increase over time because the claims adjudication processes can take many years to resolve. The 51 spills we identified, which constitute about 2 percent of all vessel spills from 1990 to 2006, varied greatly from year to year in number and cost and showed no discernible trends in frequency or size. All vessel types were involved with the 51 major spills we identified—with cargo/freight vessels and tank barges involved with 30 of the 51 spills.

Three main factors affect the costs of a spill, according to industry experts and agency officials and the studies we reviewed: the spill's location, the time of year it occurs, and the type of oil spilled [6]. A remote location, for example, can increase the cost of a spill because of the additional expense involved in mounting a remote response. Similarly, a spill that occurs close to shore rather than further out at sea can become more expensive because it may involve the use of manual labor to remove oil from sensitive shoreline habitat. Time also has situation-specific effects, in that a spill that occurs at a particular time of year might involve a much greater cost than a spill occurring in the same place but at a different time of year. For example, a spill occurring during fishing or tourist season might carry additional economic damage, or a spill occurring during a typically stormy season might prove more expensive because it is more difficult to clean up than one occurring during a season with generally calmer weather. The specific type of oil affects costs because the type of oil can affect the amount of cleanup needed and the amount of natural resource damage incurred. Lighter oils such as gasoline or diesel fuels dissipate and evaporate quickly—requiring minimal cleanup—but are highly toxic and create severe environmental impacts. Heavier oils such as crude oil do not evaporate, and therefore may require intensive structural and shoreline cleanup; and while they are less toxic than light oils, heavy oils can harm waterfowl and fur-bearing mammals through coating and ingestion. Each spill's cost reflects the particular mix of these factors, and no factor is clearly predictive of the outcome. The 51 major spills we identified, for example, occurred on all U.S. coasts, across all seasons, and with all major types of oil; but each spill's particular location, time, or product contributed to making it expensive. Although the total costs of the San Francisco spill are unknown, some of the same key factors such as location and oil type will likely have an impact on the costs of the spill.

To date, the Fund has been able to cover costs that responsible parties have not paid, but risks remain. In particular, the Fund is at risk from claims resulting from spills that significantly exceed responsible parties' liability limits. The effect of such spills can be seen among the 51 major oil spills we identified: 10 of them exceeded the limit of liability, resulting in claims of about $252 million on the Fund. In the Coast Guard and Maritime Transportation Act of 2006, the Congress increased these liability limits, but for two main reasons, additional attention to the limits appears warranted. First, the liability limits for certain vessel types may be disproportionately low compared with their historic spill cost. For example, of the 51 major spills since 1990, 15 resulted from tank barges. The average cost for these 15 tank barge spills was about $23 million— more than double the average new liability limit ($10.3 million) for these vessels. The Coast Guard is responsible for adjusting limits of liability at least every 3 years for significant increases in inflation and for making recommendations to Congress on whether adjustments to limits are necessary to help protect the Fund [7]. In its January 2007 report examining oil spills that exceeded the limits of liability, the Coast Guard had similar findings on the adequacy of some of the new limits. However, the Coast Guard did not make explicit recommendations to Congress on how the limits should be adjusted. Second, although OPA has required since 1990 that liability limits be adjusted every 3 years to account for significant increases in inflation, such adjustments have never been made. If such adjustments had been made between 1990 and 2006, claims against the fund for the 51 major spills would have been reduced by 16 percent, which could have saved the Fund $39 million. The Coast Guard, which has been delegated the authority to adjust limits for significant increases in inflation, has not indicated whether it will exercise its authority to adjust liability limits in the future. Aside from issues related to limits of liability, the Fund faces other potential drains on its resources, including ongoing claims from existing spills, claims related to already-sunken vessels that may begin to leak oil, and the threat of a catastrophic spill such as occurred with the Exxon Valdez in 1989.

In our September 2007 report, we recommended that the Commandant of the Coast Guard (1) determine whether and how liability limits should be changed, by vessel type, and make recommendations about these changes to the Congress and (2) adjust the limits of liability for vessels every 3 years to reflect changes in inflation, as appropriate. The Department of Homeland Security (DHS), including the Coast Guard, generally agreed with the report's contents and agreed with the recommendations. To date, the Commandant of the Coast Guard has not implemented these recommendations.

BACKGROUND

With more than 100,000 commercial vessels navigating U.S. waters and 12.2 million barrels of oil being imported into the United States each day, some oil spills in domestic waters are inevitable. Fortunately, however, spills are relatively infrequent and are decreasing. While oil transport and maritime traffic have continued to increase, the total number of reported spills has generally declined each year since 1990.

OPA places the primary burden of liability and the costs of oil spills on the vessel owner and operator who were responsible for the spill [8]. This "polluter pays" system provides a deterrent for vessel owners and operators who spill oil by requiring that they assume the burden of spill response, natural resource restoration, and compensation to those damaged by the spill, up to a specified limit of liability—which is the amount above which responsible parties are no longer financially liable under certain conditions. (See figure 1 for the limits of liability by vessel type.) For example, if a vessel's limit of liability is $10 million and a spill resulted in $12 million in costs, the responsible party only has to pay up to $10 million—the Fund will pay for the remaining $2 million [9]. The Coast Guard is responsible for adjusting limits for significant increases in inflation and for making recommendations to Congress on whether other adjustments are necessary to help protect the Fund [10]. OPA also requires that vessel owners and operators must demonstrate their ability to pay for oil spill response up to their limit of liability. Specifically, by regulation, with few exceptions, owners and operators of vessels over 300 gross tons and any vessels that transship or transfer oil in the Exclusive Economic Zone are required to have a certificate of financial responsibility that demonstrates their ability to pay for oil spill response up to their limit of liability [11].

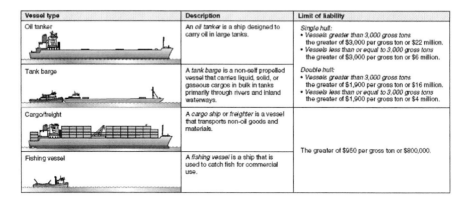

Vessel type	Description	Limit of liability
Oil tanker	An *oil tanker* is a ship designed to carry oil in large tanks.	*Single hull:* • *Vessels greater than 3,000 gross tons* the greater of $3,000 per gross ton or $22 million. • *Vessels less than or equal to 3,000 gross tons* the greater of $3,000 per gross ton or $6 million.
Tank barge	A *tank barge* is a non-self propelled vessel that carries liquid, solid, or gaseous cargos in bulk in tanks primarily through rivers and inland waterways.	*Double hull:* • *Vessels greater than 3,000 gross tons* the greater of $1,900 per gross ton or $16 million. • *Vessels less than or equal to 3,000 gross tons* the greater of $1,900 per gross ton or $4 million.
Cargo/freight	A *cargo ship* or *freighter* is a vessel that transports non-oil goods and materials.	The greater of $950 per gross ton or $800,000.
Fishing vessel	A *fishing vessel* is a ship that is used to catch fish for commercial use.	

Figure 1. Description of Vessel Types and Current Limits of Liability.

OPA consolidated the liability and compensation provisions of four prior federal oil pollution initiatives and their respective trust funds into the Oil Spill Liability Trust Fund and authorized the collection of revenue and the use of the money, with certain limitations, with regard to expenditures [12]. The Fund's balance has generally declined from 1995 through 2006, and since fiscal year 2003, its balance has been less than the authorized limit on federal expenditures for the response to a single spill, which is currently set at $1 billion (see figure 2).

The balance has declined, in part, because the Fund's main source of revenue—a $0.05 .per barrel tax on U.S. produced and imported oil—was not collected for most of the time between 1993 and 2006 [13]. As a result, the Fund balance was $604.4 million at the end of fiscal year 2006 [14]. The Energy Policy Act of 2005 reinstated the barrel tax beginning in April 2006 [15]. With the barrel tax once again in place, NPFC anticipates that the Fund will be able to cover potential noncatastrophic liabilities.

OPA also defines the costs for which responsible parties are liable and for which the Fund is made available for compensation in the event that the responsible party does not pay or is not identified. These costs, or "OPA compensable" costs, are of two main types:

- *Removal costs:* Removal costs are incurred by the federal government or any other entity taking approved action to respond to, contain, and clean up the spill. For example, removal costs include the equipment used in the response—skimmers to pull oil from the water, booms to contain the oil, planes for aerial observation—as well as salaries and travel and lodging costs for responders.

- *Damages caused by the oil spill:* OPA-compensable damages cover a wide range of both actual and potential adverse impacts from an oil spill, for which a claim may be made to either the responsible party or the Fund. Claims include natural resource damage claims filed by trustees, claims for uncompensated removal costs and third-party damage claims for lost or damaged property and lost profits, among other things [16]

The Fund also covers costs when responsible parties cannot be located or do not pay their liabilities. NPFC encounters cases where the source of the spill, and therefore the responsible party is unknown, or where the responsible party does not have the ability to pay. In other cases, since the cost recovery can take a period of years, the responsible party may become bankrupt or dissolved. Based on our analysis of NPFC records, responsible parties have reimbursed the majority—about 65 percent—of the Fund's costs for the 51 spills [17].

Response to large oil spills is typically a cooperative effort between the public and private sector, and there are numerous players who participate in responding to and paying for oil spills. To manage the response effort, the responsible party, the Coast Guard, EPA, and the pertinent state and local agencies form the unified command, which implements and manages the spill response [18]. Appendix I contains additional information on the parties involved in spill response.

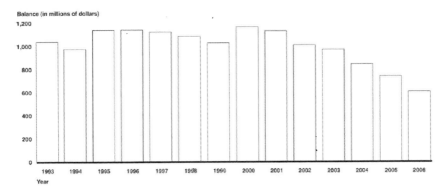

Figure 2. Oil Spill Liability Trust Fund Balance, Fiscal Years 1993-2006.

Oil Spills Costing at Least $1 Million Occurred Infrequently between 1990 and 2006, but Estimated Costs Total $860 Million to $1.1 Billion

On the basis of information we were able to assemble about responsible parties' expenditures and payments from the Fund, we estimate that 51 oil spills involving removal costs and damage claims totaling at least $1 million have occurred from 1990 to 2006. During this period, 3,389 oil spills occurred in which one or more parties sought reimbursement from the Fund. The 51 major spills represent less than 2 percent of this total [19]. As figure 3 shows, there are no discernable trends in the number of major oil spills that occur each year. The highest number of spills was seven in 1996; the lowest number was zero in 2006.

These 51 spills occurred in a variety of locations and involved a range of vessel types. The spills occurred on the Atlantic, Gulf, and Pacific coasts and include spills both in open coastal waters and inland waterways. In addition, as figure 4 shows, 30 of the 51 spills involved cargo/freight vessels and tank barges, 12 involved fishing and other types of vessels, and 9 involved tanker vessels.

The total cost of the 51 spills cannot be precisely determined because private-sector expenditures are not tracked, [20] the various parties involved in covering these costs do not categorize them uniformly, and spills costs are somewhat fluid and accrue over time. Because spill cost data are somewhat imprecise and the data we collected vary somewhat by source, the results described below will be reported in ranges, in which various data sources are combined together.

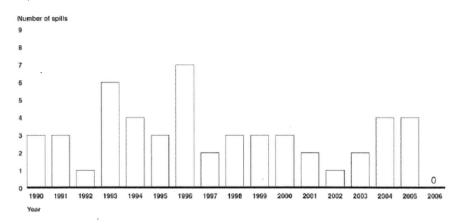

Figure 3. Number of Major Oil Spills, by Year, 1990-2006.

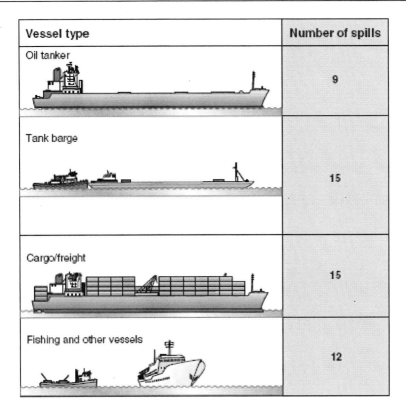

Vessel type	Number of spills
Oil tanker	9
Tank barge	15
Cargo/freight	15
Fishing and other vessels	12

Figure 4. Major Oil Spills From 1990 to 2006, By Vessel Type.

The lower and higher bounds of the range represent the low and high end of cost information we obtained Our analysis of these 51 spills shows their total cost was approximately $1 billion—ranging from $860 million to $1.1 billion. This amount breaks down by source as follows:

- *Amount paid out of the Trust Fund:* Because the NPFC tracks and reports all Fund expenditures, the amount paid from the Fund can be reported as an actual amount, not an estimate. For these 51 spills, the Fund paid a total of $239.5 million.
- *Amount paid by responsible parties:* Because of the lack of precise information about amounts paid by responsible parties and the differences in how they categorize their costs, this portion of the expenditures must be presented as an estimate. Based on the data we were able to obtain and analyze, responsible parties spent between $620

million and $840 million. Even at the low end of the range, this amount is nearly triple the expenditure from the Fund.

Costs of these 51 spills varied widely by spill, and therefore, by year (see figure 5). For example, 1994 and 2004 both had four spills during the year, but the average cost per spill in 1994 was about $30 million, while the average cost per spill in 2004 was between $71 million and $96 million. Just as there was no discernible trend in the frequency of these major spills, there is no discernible trend in their cost. Although the substantial increase in 2004 may look like an upward trend, 2004 may be an anomaly that reflects the unique character of two of the four spills that occurred that year. These two spills accounted for 98 percent of the year's costs.

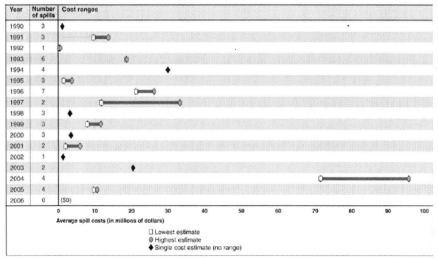

Note: Because we are reporting costs from multiple sources of data, the data were combined and grouped into cost ranges. In some cases, however, there was only one cost estimate. In those cases, we present the amount as a single cost estimate.

Figure 5. Average per Spill Costs of Major Oil Spills, by Year, 1990-2006.

KEY FACTORS AFFECT OIL SPILL COSTS IN UNIQUE WAYS

Location, time of year, and type of oil are key factors affecting oil spill costs, according to industry experts, agency officials, and our analysis of spills [21]. Officials also identified two other factors that may influence oil spill costs to a lesser extent—the effectiveness of the spill response and the level of public interest in a spill. In ways that are unique to each spill, these factors can affect the breadth and difficulty of the response effort or the extent of damage that requires mitigation.

Chapter 1

LOCATION IMPACTS COSTS IN DIFFERENT WAYS

The location of a spill can have a large bearing on spill costs because it will determine the extent of response needed, as well as the degree of damage to the environment and local economies. According to state officials with whom we spoke and industry experts, there are three primary characteristics of location that affect costs:

- *Remoteness:* For spills that occur in remote areas, spill response can be particularly difficult in terms of mobilizing responders and equipment, and they can complicate the logistics of removing oil from the water—all of which can increase the costs of a spill.
- *Proximity to shore:* There are also significant costs associated with spills that occur close to shore. Contamination of shoreline areas has a considerable bearing on the costs of spills as such spills can require manual labor to remove oil from the shoreline and sensitive habitats. The extent of damage is also affected by the specific shoreline location.
- *Proximity to economic centers:* Spills that occur in the proximity of economic centers can also result in increased costs when local services are disrupted. A spill near a port can interrupt the flow of goods, necessitating an expeditious response in order to resume business activities, which could increase removal costs. Additionally, spills that disrupt economic activities can result in expensive third-party damage claims.

TIME OF YEAR HAS IMPACT ON LOCAL ECONOMIES AND RESPONSE EFFORTS

The time of year in which a spill occurs can also affect spill costs—in particular, impacting local economies and response efforts. According to several state and private-sector officials with whom we spoke, spills that disrupt seasonal events that are critical for local economies can result in considerable expenses. For example, spills in the spring months in areas of the country that rely on revenue from tourism may incur additional removal costs in order to expedite spill clean-up, or because there are stricter standards for clean up, which increase the costs.

The time of year in which a spill occurs also affects response efforts because of possible inclement weather conditions. For example, spills that occur during the winter months in areas of the country that experience harsh winter conditions can result in higher removal costs because of the increased difficulty in mobilizing equipment and personnel to respond to a spill in inclement weather. According to a state official knowledgeable about a January 1996 spill along the coast of Rhode Island, extremely cold and stormy weather made response efforts very difficult.

Chapter 2

TYPE OF OIL SPILLED IMPACTS THE EXTENT OF THE RESPONSE EFFORT AND THE AMOUNT OF DAMAGE

The type of oil spilled affects the degree to which oil can be cleaned up and removed, as well as the nature of the natural resource damage caused by the spill. The different types of oil can be grouped into four categories, each with its own set of impacts on spill response and the environment (see table 1).

In general, oil types differ from each other in three ways: viscosity—oil's resistance to flow, volatility—how quickly the oil evaporates in the air, and toxicity—how poisonous the oil is to people and other organisms.

Lighter oils such as jet fuels, gasoline, and diesel fuel dissipate and evaporate quickly, and as such, often require minimal cleanup. However, these oils are highly toxic and can severely affect the environment if conditions for evaporation are unfavorable. For instance, in 1996, a tank barge that was carrying home-heating oil grounded in the middle of a storm near Point Judith, Rhode Island, spilling approximately 828,000 gallons of heating oil (light oil). Although this oil might dissipate quickly under normal circumstances, heavy wave conditions caused an estimated 80 percent of the release to mix with water [22]. Natural resource damages alone were estimated at $18 million, due to the death of approximately 9 million lobsters, 27 million clams and crabs, and over 4 million fish.

Heavier oils, such as crude oils and other heavy petroleum products are less toxic than lighter oils but can also have severe environmental impacts. Medium and heavy oils do not evaporate much, even during favorable weather conditions, and can blanket structures they come in contact with—boats and fishing gear, for example—as well as the shoreline, creating severe environmental impacts to these areas, and harming waterfowl and fur-bearing mammals through coating and ingestion.

Table 1. Description of Different Oil Types

Oil type	Removal and response	Environmental impact
Very light oils (Jet fuels, gasoline)	Highly volatile (they will evaporate within 1-2 days). It is rarely possible to clean up the oil from such spills.	Highly toxic: Can cause severe impacts to shoreline resources.
Light oils (Diesel, No. 2 fuel oil, light crudes)	Moderately volatile, but will leave a residue after a few days. Cleanup can be very effective for these spills.	Moderately toxic: Has the potential to create long-term contamination of shoreline resources.
Medium oils (Most crude oils)	Some oil (about one-third) will evaporate in 24 hours. Cleanup most effective if conducted quickly.	Less toxic: Oil contamination of shoreline can be severe and long-term, and can have significant impacts to waterfowl and fur-bearing mammals.
Heavy oils (Heavy crude oils, No. 6 fuel oil, bunker C fuel)	Little or no oil will evaporate. Cleanup is difficult.	Less toxic: Heavy contamination of shoreline resources is likely, with severe impacts to waterfowl and fur- bearing mammals through coating and ingestion.

Additionally, heavy oils can sink, creating prolonged contamination of the sea bed and tar balls that sink to the ocean floor and scatter along beaches. These spills can require intensive shoreline and structural clean up, which is time-consuming and expensive. For example, in 1995, a tanker spilled approximately 38,000 gallons of heavy fuel oil into the Gulf of Mexico when it collided with another tanker as it prepared to lighter its oil to another ship [23]. Less than 1 percent (210 gallons) of the oil was recovered from the sea, and as a result, recovery efforts on the beaches of Matagorda and South Padre Islands were labor intensive, as hundreds of workers had to manually pick up tar balls with shovels. The total removal costs for the spill were estimated at $7 million.

OTHER FACTORS ALSO AFFECT SPILL COSTS

Some industry experts cited two other factors as also affecting costs incurred during a spill.

- *Effectiveness of Spill Response*: Some private-sector officials stated that the effectiveness of spill response can impact the cost of cleanup. The longer it takes to assemble and conduct the spill response, the more likely it is that the oil will move with changing tides and currents and affect a greater area, which can increase costs. Some officials said the level of experience of those involved in the incident command is critical to the effectiveness of spill response. For example, they said poor decision making during a spill response could lead to the deployment of unnecessary response equipment, or worse, not enough equipment to respond to a spill. Several officials expressed concern that Coast Guard officials are increasingly inexperienced in handling spill response, in part because the Coast Guard's mission has been increased to include homeland security initiatives.
- *Public interest:* Several officials with whom we spoke stated that the level of public attention placed on a spill creates pressure on parties to take action and can increase costs. They also noted that the level of public interest can increase the standards of cleanliness expected, which may increase removal costs

KEY FACTORS WILL LIKELY INFLUENCE COST OF SAN FRANCISCO SPILL

The total costs of the San Francisco spill are currently unknown. According to NPFC officials, as of December 4, 2007, the Unified Command estimated that $48 million had been spent on the response, which includes approximately $2.2 million from the Fund [24]. The total costs will not likely be known for a while, as it can take many months or years to determine the full effect of a spill on natural resources and to determine the costs and extent of the natural resource damage. Our work for this testimony did not include a thorough evaluation of the factors affecting the spill. However, some of the same key factors that have influenced the cost of 51 major oil spills will likely have an effect on the costs in the San Francisco spill. For example, the spill occurred in an area close to shore, which caused the closing of as many as 22 beaches, according to Coast Guard officials. A weather-related factor was that the spill occurred during dense fog, which complicated efforts to determine how much of an area the spill covered. Moreover, the cargo ship spilled a heavy oil—specifically intermediate fuel oil— that requires particularly intensive shoreline and structural clean-up, and harmed scores of birds and marine mammals through coating and ingestion [25]. Concerns have also been raised about the effectiveness of the spill response and incident command, another of the factors cited as contributing to increased costs. The National Transportation Safety Board, the Coast Guard, as well as other government agencies, are currently investigating the details of the accident and the subsequent response.

Chapter 3

FUND HAS BEEN ABLE TO COVER COSTS NOT PAID BY RESPONSIBLE PARTIES, BUT RISKS REMAIN

The Fund has been able to cover costs from major spills that responsible parties have not paid, but risks remain. Specifically, the current liability limits for certain vessel types, notably tank barges, may be disproportionately low relative to costs associated with such spills. There is also no assurance that vessel owners and operators are able to financially cover these new limits, because the Coast Guard has not yet issued regulations for satisfying financial responsibility requirements. In addition, although OPA calls for periodic increases in liability limits to account for significant increases in inflation, such increases have never been made. Aside from issues related to limits of liability, the Fund faces other potential drains on its resources, including ongoing claims from existing spills.

FURTHER ATTENTION TO LIMITS OF LIABILITY IS NEEDED

The Fund has been able to cover costs from major spills that responsible parties have not paid, but additional focus on limits of liability is warranted. Limits of liability are the amount, under certain circumstances, above which responsible parties are no longer financially liable for spill removal costs and damage claims. If the responsible party's costs exceed the limit of liability, they can make a claim against the Fund for the amount above the limit. Major oil spills that exceed a vessel's limit of liability are infrequent, but their impact on the Fund can be significant. Ten of the 51 major oil spills that occurred since 1990 resulted in limit of liability claims on the Fund [26]. These limit-of-liability claims totaled more than $252 million and ranged from less than $1 million to more than $100 million. Limit-of-liability claims will continue to have a pronounced effect on the Fund. NPFC estimates that 74 percent of claims under adjudication that were outstanding as of January 2007 were for spills in which the limit of liability had been exceeded. The amount of these claims under adjudication was $217 million [27].

We identified three areas in which further attention to these liability limits appears warranted: the appropriateness of some current liability limits, the need to adjust limits periodically in the future to account for significant increases in inflation, and the need for updated regulations for ensuring vessel owners and operators are able to financially cover their new limits.

Chapter 4

SOME RECENT ADJUSTMENTS TO LIABILITY LIMITS DO NOT REFLECT THE COST OF MAJOR SPILLS

The Coast Guard and Maritime Transportation Act of 2006 significantly increased the limits of liability from the limits set by OPA in 1990. Both laws base the liability on a specified amount per gross ton of vessel volume, with different amounts for vessels that transport oil commodities (tankers and tank barges) than for vessels that carry oil as a fuel (such as cargo vessels, fishing vessels, and passenger ships). The 2006 act raised both the per-ton and the required minimum amounts, differentiating between vessels with a double hull, which helps prevent oil spills resulting from collision or grounding, and vessels without a double hull (see table 2 for a comparison of amounts by vessel category) [28]. For example, the liability limit for single-hull vessels larger than 3,000 gross tons was increased from the greater of $1,200 per gross ton or $10 million to the greater of $3,000 per gross ton or $22 million.

Our analysis of the 51 spills showed that the average spill cost for some types of vessels, particularly tank barges, was higher than the limit of liability, including the new limits established in 2006. As figure 6 shows, the 15 tank barge spills and the 12 fishing/other vessel spills had average costs greater than both the 1990 and 2006 limits of liability. For example, for tank barges, the average cost of $23 million was higher than the average limit of liability of $4.1 million under the 1990 limits and $10.3 million under the new 2006 limits. The nine spills involving tankers, by comparison, had average spill costs of $34 million, which was considerably lower than the average limit of liability of $77 million under the 1990 limits and $187 million under the new 2006 limits. [29].

Table 2. Comparison of Limits of Liability as Established in OPA (1990) and the Coast Guard and Maritime Transportation Act (2006)

Vessel types	1990 Limit of liability	2006 Limit of liability
Single-hull tankersand tank barges	Vesselsgreater than 3,000 grosstons: the greater of $1,200 per grosston or $10 million.	Vesselsgreater than 3,000 grosstons: the greater of $3,000 per grosston or $22 million.
	Vesselslessthan or equal to 3,000 grosstons: the greater of $1,200 per grosston or $2 million	Vesselslessthan or equal to 3,000 grosstons: the greater of $3,000 per grosston or $6 million.
	(Single and double-hull tankersand tank barges.)	
Double-hull tankersand tank barges	Vesselsgreater than 3,000 grosstons: the greater of $1,200 per grosston or $10 million.	Vesselsgreater than 3,000 grosstons: the greater of $1,900 per grosston or $16 million.
	Vesselslessthan or equal to 3,000 grosstons: the greater of $1,200 per grosston or $2 million	Vesselslessthan or equal to 3,000 grosstons:the greater of $1,900 per grosston or $4 million.
	(Single and double-hull tankersand tank barges.)	
All other vessels: Cargo vessels, fishing vessels, passenger ships	The greater of $600 per grosston or $500,000.	The greater of $950 per grosston or $800,000.

Source: Coast Guard and Maritime Transportation Act of 2006.

Similarly, the 15 major spills involving cargo/freight vessels had an average spill cost of $67 million, which was lower than both the 1990 and 2006 limits of liability.

In a January 2007 report examining spills in which the limits of liability had been exceeded, the Coast Guard had similar findings on the adequacy of some of the new limits [30]. Based on an analysis of 40 spills in which costs had exceeded the responsible party's liability limit since 1991, the Coast Guard found that the Fund's responsibility would be greatest for spills involving tank barges, where the Fund would be responsible for paying 69 percent of costs.

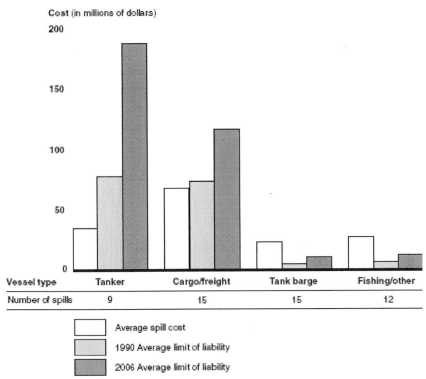

Source: GAO.

Figure 6. Average Spill Costs and Limits of Liability for Major Oil Spill Vessels, 1990-2006.

The Coast Guard concluded that increasing liability limits for tank barges and non tank vessels—cargo, freight, and fishing vessels— over 300 gross tons would positively impact the Fund balance. With regard to making specific adjustments, the Coast Guard said dividing costs equally between the responsible parties and the Fund was a reasonable standard to apply in determining the adequacy of liability limits [31]. However, the Coast Guard did not recommend explicit changes to achieve either that 50/50 standard or some other division of responsibility.

Chapter 5

LIABILITY LIMITS HAVE NOT BEEN ADJUSTED FOR INFLATION

Although OPA requires adjusting liability limits to account for significant increases in inflation, no adjustments to the limits were made between 1990 and 2006, when the Congress raised the limits in the Coast Guard and Maritime Transportation Act. During those years, the Consumer Price Index rose approximately 54 percent [32]. OPA requires the President, who has delegated responsibility to the Coast Guard, through the Secretary of Homeland Security, to issue regulations not less often than every 3 years to adjust the limits of liability to reflect significant increases in the Consumer Price Index [33]. We asked Coast Guard officials why no adjustments were made between 1990 and 2006. Coast Guard officials stated that they could not speculate on behalf of other agencies as to why no adjustments had been made prior to 2005 when the delegation to the Coast Guard was made [34]

The decision to leave limits unchanged had financial implications for the Fund. Raising the liability limits to account for inflation would have the effect of reducing payments from the Fund, because responsible parties would be responsible for paying costs up to the higher liability limit. Not making adjustments during this 16-year period thus had the effect of increasing the Fund's financial liability. Our analysis showed that if the 1990 liability limits had been adjusted for inflation during the 16-year period, claims against the Fund for the 51 major oil spills would have been reduced 16 percent, from $252 million to $213 million. This would have meant a savings of $39 million for the Fund.

Chapter 6

CERTIFICATION OF COMPLIANCE WITH THE NEW LIABILITY LIMITS IS NOT IN PLACE

Certificates of Financial Responsibility have not been adjusted to reflect the new liability limits. The Coast Guard requires Certificates of Financial Responsibility, with few exceptions, for vessels over 300 gross tons or any vessels that are lightering or transshipping oil in the Exclusive Economic Zone as a legal certification that vessel owners and operators have the financial resources to fund spill response up to the vessel's limit of liability. Currently, Certificate of Financial Responsibility requirements are consistent with the 1990 limits of liability and, therefore, there is no assurance that responsible parties have the financial resources to cover their increased liability [35]. The Coast Guard plans to initiate a rule making to issue new Certificate of Financial Responsibility requirements. Coast Guard officials indicated their goal is to publish a Notice of Proposed Rulemaking by the end of 2007, but they said they could not be certain they would meet this goal.

Chapter 7

OTHER CHALLENGES COULD ALSO AFFECT THE FUND'S CONDITION

The Fund also faces several other potential challenges that could affect its financial condition:

- *Additional claims could be made on spills that have already been cleaned up:* Natural resource damage claims can be made on the Fund for years after a spill has been cleaned up. The official natural resource damage assessment conducted by trustees can take years to complete, and once it is completed, claims can be submitted to the NPFC for up to 3 years thereafter [36]. For example, NPFC recently received and paid a natural resource damage claim for a spill in U.S. waters in the Caribbean that occurred in 1991.
- *Costs and claims may occur on spills from previously sunken vessels that discharge oil in the future*: Previously sunken vessels that are submerged and in threat of discharging oil represent an ongoing liability to the Fund. There are over 1000 sunken vessels that pose a threat of oil discharge [37]. These potential spills are particularly problematic because in many cases there is no viable responsible party that would be liable for removal costs. Therefore, the full cost burden of oil spilled from these vessels would likely be paid by the Fund.
- *Spills may occur without an identifiable source and therefore, no responsible party:* Mystery spills also have a sustained impact on the Fund, because costs for spills without an identifiable source—and therefore no responsible party—may be paid out of the Fund. Although mystery spills are a concern, the total cost to the Fund from mystery spills was lower than the costs of known vessel spills in 2001 through 2004.

Additionally, none of the 51 major oil spills was the result of discharge from an unknown source.

- *A catastrophic spill could strain the Fund's resources:* Since the 1989 Exxon Valdez spill, which was the impetus for authorizing the Fund's usage, no oil spill has come close to matching its costs [38]. Cleanup costs for the Exxon Valdez alone totaled about $2.2 billion, according to the vessel's owner. By comparison, the 51 major oil spills since 1990 cost, in total, between $860 million and $1.1 billion. The Fund is currently authorized to pay out a maximum of $1 billion on a single spill. Although the Fund has been successful thus far in covering costs that responsible parties did not pay, it may not be sufficient to pay such costs for a spill that has catastrophic consequences.

Chapter 8

CONCLUDING OBSERVATIONS

In conclusion, the "polluter pays" system established under OPA has been generally effective in ensuring that responsible parties pay the costs of responding to spills and compensating those affected. However, increases in some liability limits appear warranted to help ensure that the "polluter pays" principle is carried out in practice. For certain vessel types, such as tank barges, current liability limits appear disproportionately low relative to their historic spill costs. The Coast Guard has reached a similar conclusion but so far has stopped short of making explicit recommendations to the Congress about what the limits should be Absent such recommendations, the Fund may continue to pay tens of millions for spills that exceed the responsible parties' limits of liability. Further, to date, liability limits have not been regularly adjusted for significant changes in inflation. Consequently, the Fund was exposed to about $39 million in liability claims for the 51 major spills between 1990 and 2006 that could have been saved if the limits had been adjusted for inflation. Without such actions, oil spills with costs exceeding the responsible parties' limits of liability will continue to place the Fund at risk. Given these concerns, in our September 2007 report, we recommended that the Commandant of the Coast Guard (1) determine whether and how liability limits should be changed, by vessel type, and make recommendations about these changes to the Congress and (2) adjust the limits of liability for vessels every 3 years to reflect significant changes in inflation, as appropriate. DHS, including the Coast Guard, generally agreed with the report's contents and agreed with the recommendations. To date, the Commandant of the Coast Guard has not implemented these recommendations.

Madame Chair this concludes my statement. I would be pleased to answer any questions that you or other Members of the Subcommittee may have at this time.

APPENDIX I:
INFORMATION ON SPILL RESPONSE

Response to large oil spills is typically a cooperative effort between the public and private sector, and there are numerous players who participate in responding to and paying for oil spills. To manage the response effort, the responsible party, the Coast Guard, EPA, and the pertinent state and local agencies form the unified command, which implements and manages the spill response [1]. Beyond the response operations, there are other stakeholders, such as accountants who are involved in documenting and accounting for costs, and receiving and processing claims. In addition, insurers and underwriters provide financial backing to the responsible party. The players involved in responding to and/or paying for major spill response are as follows: [2]

Government agencies: The lead federal authority, or Federal On-Scene Coordinator, in conducting a spill response is usually the nearest Coast Guard Sector and is headed by the Coast Guard Captain of the Port [3]. The Federal On-Scene Coordinator directs response efforts and coordinates all other efforts at the scene of an oil spill. Additionally, the on-scene coordinator issues pollution removal funding authorizations—guarantees that the agency will receive reimbursement for performing response activities—to obtain services and assistance from other government agencies. Other federal agencies may also be involved. NOAA provides scientific support, monitoring and predicting the movement of oil, and conducting environmental assessments of the impacted area. The federal, state, and tribal trustees join together to perform a natural resource damage assessment, if necessary. Within the Coast Guard, the NPFC is responsible for disbursing funds to the federal on-scene coordinator for oil spill removal activities and seeking reimbursement from responsible parties for federal costs. Additionally, regional governmental entities that are affected by the spill—

both state and local—as well as tribal government officials or representatives may participate in the unified command and contribute to the response effort, which is paid for by the responsible party or are reimbursed by the responsible party or the Fund [4].

Responsible parties: OPA stipulates that both the vessel owner and operator are ultimately liable for the costs of the spill and the cleanup effort. The Coast Guard has final determination on what actions must be taken in a spill response, and the responsible party may form part of the unified command—along with the federal on-scene coordinator and pertinent state and local agencies—to manage the spill response. The responsible parties rely on other entities to evaluate the spill effects and the resulting compensation. Responsible parties hire environmental and scientific support staff, specialized claims adjustors to adjudicate third- party claims, public relations firms, and legal representation to file and defend limit of liability claims on the Fund, as well as serve as counsel throughout the spill response.

Qualified individuals: Federal regulations require that vessels carrying oil as cargo have an incident response plan and, as part of the plan, they appoint a qualified individual who acts with full authority to obligate funds required to carry out response activities. The qualified individual acts as a liaison with the Federal On-Scene Coordinator and is responsible for activating the incident response plan.

Oil spill response organizations: These organizations are private companies that perform oil spill cleanup, such as skimming and disposal of oil. Many of the companies have contractual agreements with responsible parties and the Coast Guard. The agreements, called basic ordering agreements, provide for prearranged pricing, response personnel, and equipment in the event of an oil spill.

Insurers: Responsible parties often have multiple layers of primary and excess insurance coverage, which pays oil spill costs and claims. Pollution liability coverage for large vessels is often underwritten by not-for-profit mutual insurance organizations. The organizations act as a collective of ship owners, who insure themselves, at-cost. The primary insurers of commercial vessels in U.S. waters are the Water Quality Insurance.

Syndicate, an organization providing pollution liability insurance to over 40,000 vessels, and the International Group of P & I Clubs, 13 protection and indemnity organizations that provide insurance primarily to foreign- flagged large vessels [5].

At the federal level, the National Oil and Hazardous Substances Pollution Contingency Plan provides the framework for responding to oil spills [6]. At the port level, each port has an Area Contingency Plan, developed by a committee of local stakeholders, that calls for a response that is coordinated with both higher-level federal plans and lower-level facility and vessel plans. The federal plans designate the Coast Guard as the primary agency to respond to oil spills on water. The Coast Guard has a National Strike Force to provide assistance to efforts by the local Coast Guard and other agencies [7]. The Coast Guard also has an exercise program—known as the Spills of National Significance exercise program—to test national level response capabilities. This program is focused on exercising the entire response system as the local, regional and national level using large-scale, high probability oil and hazardous material incidents that result from unintentional causes such as maritime accidents or natural disasters. The most recent program exercise, in June 2007, tested the response and recovery to an oil and hazardous materials release in the wake of a large scale earthquake in the Mississippi and Ohio river valleys.

REFERENCES

[1] As of December 4, 2007, about 20,000 gallons of oil had been recovered.

[2] Responsible parties are liable without limit, however, if the oil discharge is the result of gross negligence, or a violation of federal operation, safety, and construction regulations.

[3] The National Oil and Hazardous Substances Pollution Contingency Plan states that any oil discharge that poses a substantial threat to public health or welfare of the United States or the environment or results in significant public concern shall be classified as a major spill. For the purposes of our work, however, we defined major spills as spills with total removal costs and damage claims that exceed $1 million.

[4] GAO, *Maritime Transportation: Major Oil Spills Occur Infrequently, but Risks to the Federal Oil Spill Fund Remain*, GAO-07-1085 (Washington, D.C.: Sept. 7, 2007). The Coast Guard and Maritime Transportation Act of 2006 directed us to conduct an assessment of the cost of response activities and claims related to oil spills from vessels that have occurred since January 1, 1990, for which the total costs and claims paid was at least $1 million per spill. The mandate required that the report summarize the costs and claims for oil spills that have occurred since January 1, 1990, that total at least $1 million per spill, and the source, if known, of each spill for each year.

[5] Environmental Research Consulting is a private consulting firm that specializes in data analysis, environmental risk assessment, cost analyses, expert witness research and testimony, and development of comprehensive databases on oil and chemical spills in service to regulatory agencies, nongovernmental organizations, and industry.

[6] Another potential factor is the size of the spill. Although a larger spill will require an extensive and expensive cleanup effort, officials reported that

compared with the factors presented here, spill volume is less important to the costs of oil spill response.

[7] OPA has required since 1990 that the President— and through several delegations to the Secretaries of Transportation and Homeland Security and a redelegation to the Coast Guard in 2005—adjust liability limits at least every 3 years to account for significant increases in inflation. However, the executive branch has never made such adjustments.

[8] OPA applies to oil discharged from vessels or facilities into navigable waters of the United States and adjoining shorelines. OPA also covers substantial threats of discharge, even if an actual discharge does not occur.

[9] When responsible parties' costs exceed their limit of liability and the limit is upheld— because there was no gross negligence or violations of federal regulations by the vessel owner or operator—the responsible party is entitled to file a claim on the Fund to be reimbursed for costs in excess of the limit. NPFC reviews the claim to determine which costs are OPA-compensable and the responsible party is reimbursed from the Fund.

[10] Title VI of the Coast Guard and Maritime Transportation Act of 2006. Public Law 109-241, § 603 (c)(3).

[11] 33 C.F.R. §138. The U.S. Exclusive Economic Zone extends 200 nautical miles offshore.

[12] The prior federal laws regarding oil pollution included the Federal Water Pollution Control Act, the Deepwater Port Act, the Trans-Alaska Pipeline System Authorization Act, and the Outer Continental Shelf Lands Act Amendments of 1978. Congress created the Fund in 1986 but did not authorize collection of revenue or use of the money until it passed OPA in 1990.

[13] The tax expired in December 1994. Besides the barrel tax, the Fund also receives revenue in the form of interest on the Fund's principal and fines and penalties.

[14] Recent related GAO products include GAO, *U.S. Coast Guard National Pollution Funds Center: Improvements Are Needed in Internal Control Over Disbursements, GAO-04-340R (Washington, D.C.: Jan. 13, 2004) and GAO, U.S. Coast Guard National Pollution Funds Center: Claims Payment Process Was Functioning Effectively, but Additional Controls Are Needed to Reduce the Risk of Improper Payments,* GAO-04-114R (Washington, D.C.: Oct. 3, 2003).

[15] The Energy Policy Act of 2005. Public Law 109-58 § 1361. The barrel tax is scheduled to be in place until 2014.

[16] OPA authorizes the United States, states, and Indian Tribes to act on behalf of the public as natural resource trustees for natural resources under their respective trusteeship. Trustees often have information and technical expertise about the biological effects of pollution, as well as the location of sensitive species and habitats that can assist the federal on-scene coordinator in characterizing the nature and extent of site-related contamination and impacts. Federal Trustees include Commerce, DOI, the Departments of Agriculture, Defense, Energy, and other agencies authorized to manage or protect natural resources.

[17] Our analysis excluded the spills with limit of liability claims.

[18] The Incident Command System (ICS) is a standardized response management system that is part of the National Interagency Incident Management System. The ICS is organizationally flexible so that it can expand and contract to accommodate spill responses of various sizes. The ICS typically consists of four sections: operations, planning, logistics, and finance/administration.

[19] We established the universe of major oil spills from 1990 to 2006, based on available public and private sector data in consultation with NPFC, Environmental Research Consulting, and other industry experts. Additionally, we gathered removal costs and damage claims data from federal agencies involved in spill response, claims payments, and conducting natural resource damage assessments (Coast Guard, NOAA, DOI, and FWS); and to the best of our ability, we gathered private-sector cost data from vessels insurers, and in contract with Environmental Research Consulting.

[20] Under regulation S-K, 17 C.F.R. 229, companies that are publicly traded must disclose any outstanding liabilities, including liabilities such as oil spill removal costs or claims made against the company for natural resource or third-party damages incurred. However, many vessel owners or operators are not publicly traded companies

[21] Another potential factor is the size of the spill. Although a larger spill will require an extensive and expensive cleanup effort, officials reported that compared with the factors presented here, spill volume is less important to the costs of oil spill response.

[22] National Research Council of the National Academies, *Oil in the Sea III: Inputs, Fates, and Effects* (Washington, D.C.: 2003).

[23] Lightering is the process of transferring oil at sea from a very large or ultra-large carrier to smaller tankers that are capable of entering the port.

[24]   According to NPFC officials, the OPA limit of liability for this vessel, if the limit applies under the circumstances of the spill, is approximately $61.8 million.

[25]   Intermediate fuel oil is a common diesel fuel used to power marine vessels.

[26]   Additional spills had costs in excess of the vessel's limit of liability, but either the limit was not upheld or no claim was filed by the responsible party.

[27]   This figure is based on all spills with claims on the Fund, currently under adjudication, not just the 51 major spills. U.S. Coast Guard, Report on Oil Pollution Act Liability Limits, Jan. 5, 2007. Like our report, the Coast Guard's report was prepared in response to a provision in the Coast Guard and Maritime Transportation Act.

[28]   OPA requires that all tank vessels (greater than 5,000 gross tons) constructed (or that undergo major conversions) under contracts awarded after June 30, 1990, operating in U.S. navigable waters must have double hulls. Of the 51 major oil spills, all 24 major spills from tank vessels (tankers and tank barges) involved single-hull vessels.

[29]   The average limits of liability for the spills involving tankers are much greater than the average liability for tank barges because the liability is based on the volume of the vessel, and tankers generally have much higher volumes than tank barges.

[30]   U.S. Coast Guard, *Report on Oil Pollution Act Liability Limits*, Jan. 5, 2007.

[31]   We did not assess the reasonableness of adopting such a standard in determining liability limits.

[32]   The new limits, which increased an average of 125 percent for the 51 vessels involved in major oil spills, were substantially higher than the rise in inflation during the period.

[33]   Congress reiterated this requirement in the Coast Guard and Maritime Transportation Act by requiring that regulations be issued 3 years after the enactment of the act (July 11, 2006) and every 3 years afterward to adjust the limits of liability to reflect significant increases in the Consumer Price Index.

[34]   OPA has required since 1990 that the President— and through several delegations to the Secretaries of Transportation and Homeland Security and a redelegation to the Coast Guard in 2005—adjust liability limits at least every 3 years to account for significant increases in inflation. However, the executive branch has never made such adjustments.

[35]   According to the NPFC, while liable parties are not required to establish an ability to pay at the higher amended limits until the certificate of financial

responsibility rule is published as required by OPA, those parties are liable for the higher amounts.

[36] Federal response costs for spills that resulted from hurricanes Katrina and Rita were paid from the Stafford Act Disaster Relief Funds. However, private parties can seek reimbursement from the Fund for cleanup costs and damages in the future. According to NPFC, it is difficult to estimate future liabilities to the Fund as a result of hurricanes Katrina and Rita, but as of July 2007, there are no claims pending in connection with these hurricanes.

[37] Michel, J., D. Etkin, T. Gilbert, J. Waldron, C. Blocksidge, and R. Urban; 2005. *Potentially Polluting Wrecks in Marine Waters: An Issue Paper Prepared for the 2005 International Oil Spill Conference.*

[38] The Exxon Valdez only discharged about 20 percent of the oil it was carrying. A catastrophic spill from a vessel could result in costs that exceed those of the Exxon Valdez, particularly if the entire contents of a tanker were released in a 'worst-case discharge' scenario.

Appendix

[1] The Incident Command System (ICS) is a standardized response management system that is part of the National Interagency Incident Management System. The ICS is organizationally flexible so that it can expand and contract to accommodate spill responses of various sizes. The ICS typically consists of four sections: operations, planning, logistics, and finance/administration.

[2] For a full description of the organizational structure and procedures for preparing for and responding to discharges of oil, see The National Oil and Hazardous Substances Pollution Contingency Plan, 40 C.F.R. § 300.

[3] Although this report focuses on vessels, and most vessel spills are in the Coast Guard zone of jurisdiction, EPA is the lead on-scene coordinator in the inland zone, and Coast Guard is lead on-scene coordinator in the coastal zone.

[4] State governments can seek reimbursement directly from responsible parties or from the Fund. State officials in Alaska, California, New York, Rhode Island, Texas, and Washington said that state agencies recover almost all of their costs, either directly from responsible parties or from the NPFC. Officials in Texas said that the reimbursement rate for oil spill costs may be as high as 98 percent.

[5] These 13 organizations are American Steamship Owners Mutual Protection and Indemnity Association, Inc.; Assuranceforeningen Gard; Assuranceforeningen Skuld; the Britannia Steam Ship Insurance Association Limited; the Japan Ship Owners' Mutual Protection & Indemnity Association; the London Steam-Ship Owners' Mutual Insurance Association Limited; the North of England Protection and Indemnity Association, Limited; the Shipowners' Mutual Protection and Indemnity Association (Luxembourg); the Standard Steamship Owners' Protection and Indemnity Association (Bermuda), Limited; the Steamship Mutual Underwriting Association (Bermuda), Limited; the Swedish Club; United Kingdom Mutual Steam Ship Assurance Association (Bermuda), Limited; the West of England Ship Owners Mutual Insurance Association (Luxembourg).

[6] The National Oil and Hazardous Substances Pollution Contingency Plan is a part of a larger plan known as the National Response Plan which covers a wide variety of contingencies that include natural disasters, major disasters, and terrorist attacks.

[7] The National Strike Force was established in 1973. Originally comprised of three 17- member strike teams, today's National Strike Force totals over 200 active duty, civilian, and reserve Coast Guard personnel for three distinct regions—the Atlantic, Gulf and Pacific.

INDEX

W

water, 20, 27, 30, 51
waterfowl, 16, 30, 31

waterways, 21
welfare, 53
wildlife, 11
winter, 28
workers, 31